KIVA

KIVA

E. G. BURROWS

for Marjorie Rowen
E. G. Burrows

ITHACA HOUSE
1976

Also by E. G. Burrows

The Arctic Tern

Man Fishing

Thanks to the following publications in which a number of these poems originally appeared: *Anon, Ash Tree, American Poetry Review, Greenfield Review, Loon, Michigan Quarterly Review, Poetry Now, Seneca Review, Southern Poetry Review,* and *The New Moon*.

ISBN 0-87886-077-0
108 North Plain Street
Ithaca, New York

Ithaca House books are distributed by Serendipity Books, 1790 Shattuck Avenue, Berkeley, CA 94709.

For Beth

Contents

I

U.S. 29

Gates face the ditch.
There are no gates against
the waters of grass.
The road flows through a molten scrub.
It is forty miles to Miami.

Behind the feather pines
and the gates of wire
their board shacks rise
in legends and egrets
at the edge of the last interior.

On the fence a dead moccasin
hangs in the shape of omega.
It is forty miles to Miami.
Runt oaks on the hammocks
stoop like ruined gates.

A people have come to the road.
They will not cross the ditch.
Their hands are like roots
that have reached into the water
for land not there.

A people float on the grass
in the shadow of finality.
Their shacks lean.
They have closed a broken gate
with twists of Indian silver.

At night the city
stalks the road and bent scrub.
Lift your nose.
You can smell it in the ditch.
It whines at the locked gate.

Where are the people gone?
They went into the grass.
They followed the owl
and hover like gentle lights
over the fetid marsh.

In Parfrey's Glen

Without warning, the rocks arrived.
Overnight they were here
without wheelmarks. The stevedores
never left their wives.

The rocks settled like fowl.
Some toppled into the gorge
and lie staring,
waiting to be restored.
If this was a battle, we slept well.
No one heard a door close.

We go out to war
to avoid the death afterward
between two people.
We tremble at the calm of stone
where nothing is written,
not even "Faithful" or "Beloved."

We walk around them:
rocks recently breathing.
They are larger than buffalo.
Something returns,
moves inches behind our backs,
wary, huge,
boulders on edge
unable to conceal their odors.

Kettle Moraine

The moraine spine is yellow
with gleanings of grass.
A whole meadow lies on its side.
Oaks, in scooped hollow, are bronze.

Children come toward us, become us.
Children make us of the late blue flower
and farm fence with its one wire going nowhere.
Of green there is a coming absence.

The sky is faultless with October,
the fields turned down for a mongrel's frolic.
Gates open and open
under hands that meet us halfway.

Ice raised this crest.
Robins flock in the kettles of a glacial thaw.
We are bone and bone with the old men
whose pitted flints are listening like toys.

A Dream of Wisconsin

Cri, cri, roche cri.
Why do the rocks rant?
I saw in a wood cement horses
and a man made of bottles and stained glass.

The boondock lout came riding
to kill him a Sauk.
Cri, cri, roche cri.
Red wine for his eyes, the cowherd rosé.

Fifty Apostles crowd off-shore
for a breach in the wall of heathen.
Cement man with one whiskey father
stands stiff in the pines of concrete.

What do the stones cry?
A talon is nailed to the last eagle tree.
I saw in a wood a carriage
of church panes, and a coachman

blue as the Mother of God.

De Tocqueville at Memphis

Ice grinds the low gates.
I hear midstream
hump and thrash of the white
nation of buffalo.

My sleep is choked
with the grim sound of herds
tumbling over a cliff
into winter Arkansas.

The Choctaw cross here.
Threadbare,
they pass over the ice
a few deaths at a time.

They are bound
for the ovens of sparse grass,
cattle wire and antelope skulls.

Two rivers intersect.
Ice will melt in the Gulf
while the last high civilizations
go under the gun.

Corkscrew Swamp

In this place of the oldest heat
mirrors show me dense life.
I walk on the lettuce leaf
like an insect or limpkin
and I look into the mirrors of pond growth
for a face I can trust,
some ancient I can count on
who escaped the king of the bandsaws.

Old man, I know your bald tree.
It climbs with a light at sundown
to direct great storks to roost.
Your eye is orchid.
Your mouth speaks in the marsh
the husky sputter of gallinules.
How can you know me in these clothes?
I wear streets.

A city is there just behind me
at the edge of the duckweed.
Cement leaks into my shoes.
I am anchored
in the same old running dream
unable to rise,
unable to fly off in a scarlet form.
I pray to be made inhuman.

The Center

Indians fool you. They pull your leg.
Having suffered so long
they become deadpan jokers.
Imagine them sending me all the way to Kansas
for gold
when my name was Coronado.
I always find the same huts
and the same poor
in the place they say help yourself
to the treasure.

Oh, they are sly.
They flutter off with the broken wing walk
of a mother killdeer
till the piteous cry ends in a chuckle
and you are farther than ever
from the real sorrow.

Before I went there,
I believed the center of the round world
was somewhere near Pueblo Bonito.
They swore it was truth
and showed me the mouth of the rock
and a rung
from the ladder that goes down.
I have gone down.
I have looked throgh the hole in the sky.
I have talked with the whippoorwill.
The center was not there.
I know they have kept it within them
like the pit of hunger
and I cry for them like a fool.

II

Eden Revisited

The facedown signs
send words toward water.
Grass hears the fallen writing.

I leap "Keep Out."
My heel grinds
the curled serifs of "Beware."

I thought a sword burned at this gate.
Was it only a word
clanged at our backs?

An old man
was shouting like a jaybird
from the top of the apple tree.

Entries

I

It is too cold today for the trees to touch.
The sky will not turn.
Smoke spills over the roof with the odor
of pillows and lettuce.
An eye will open and shatter it all.
It is too cold for hands
or the old nest that creaks like a cinder.

II

Voices come down the stair.
They pass through the white door
and are lost in collars.
I will paint the door blue, set a sun
in the ripe half moon of glass
over the doorway. I have plans for the walls,
those paths of mice and faces
locked in the stucco wash.
I will take them apart like grass
and grow melons under the stair.

III

Home is the road where I am,
not pitched in a sweet country
but dry
and rounding a hillside
like a bee to the one farther flower.
The Chinese mountain
unrolls into vapor and the final
bones of rare linen.
I will return to the place I have never been.

Anxieties of April

The woman sleeps. There is no horizon.
Trees gnash at trees. The kettle coughs.

Morning has come again with its bundle of tremors
and the dislocation of stars.

Day hangs like an axe
on old hooks over the door.
I want to thread myself
into the eye of the smallest people.

The lake is gone that last night
spread into the cellars of ground squirrels.
Does water climb back?

If there had been angels on those ladders,
I should have heard them.

At Twenty

I cowered from old age.
My hand flew to my hair.
I threatened to break apart like old books.
I could fight Nazis.

Those cars were really old cars.
I can prove it now on TV.
I still wonder what girls were like
under those long skirts.

Old men I avoided.
Their bones bracketed me like artillery.
Now the young advance in their qualms
and I am still the same coward.

I turn up my collar and sink
into a doorway like a derelict.
I am the ageless assassin
with a stocking face.

South Haven

The lake bluff descends in scars
and kids' heel marks.
Three pines fell
with the summer children of Chicago.

Through the Shores
where a paper castle of wasps
hangs from the boarded fruitstand
you rode a warm horse.

Now doves
nest in a tire rim
and the tired blossoms close
on the silence of iron and china.

We can still sit
by the smokehouse at Black River
and shell shrimp,
though the taste makes you distant
and you lick the grease
from your fingers until they shine.

Objet D'Art

The wire grouse on his driftwood perch
never drums. He guards
this grey house with the grace
of a bent coathanger.

He is most like a cage set
to catch claws and eyes-on-a-stalk
of the sun rising crabwise,

though the soldered lozenges
of his metal bones
form a domed planetarium
to hang stars in.

He will not sing
or light up like a radio,
but I will climb through his windows before dawn
to work his wire wings.

Blue

Along the uncut
county road blue lines
are drawn up: weeds
waist high in the fogs of petroleum,
a straggle
of the "embattled" in blue ranks.
The name of that color should be
colonial.
I can't remember the real sky.

In some disemboweled mountain
a war room
keeps on file the exact hues,
each sealed with its designation
in an airless capsule.
But when the vaults are sprung
will our eyes know the language?

Already we grope
by acid on the leaf
and name birds by the air they disturb,
though sometimes a child sings
lupine and lazuli
in a nonsense rhyme.

The Farm

Waking to ice in the pail
he went out
to sweep fog from the doorstep.
On each branch of hemlock a web
sagged with its catch
and every bush wore
the folds of its Monday clothing.
My father grew small.
I narrowed my father in a child's hands
to the width of a chicken run.
The fire would come down that fire break
like the fog-burning sun to devour him.
I leaned my chin on the sill
and saw my face bloom
in the thickets of frost.
What's out there worth bringing in?

Pictograph

The black word of the Japanese
hangs with its tilted hallways
and curled eaves
framed on the wall of my room.
Ark of scraps
or imperial ruin the word
lures with its faulty stair
and attic
of indigenous swallows.

In Wisconsin
rooms wrap a stone finger
the river left wet
and testing the wind: House
on the Rock, a man's maze
of ascending campsites,
stone hewn to a honeycomb.
The symbols accrete.
The years each husk with its gable
pile on till the whole babel leans
over the gorge
and we climb the teak beams and knuckles
of one statement muttering
our own gibberish
like Polo at the throne of jade.

Pheasant Run

Flies attack. You fight back
with a long hand fanning your hair.
I beat a dead stump
for the owl who sleeps elsewhere.

A nettle's in your shoe
and every gnat darts
from the heart of the singing tornado
to taunt you.

Your eyes fray.
Have you humor enough?
Love, I am stung
by a small yellow bird.
I thrive on rages
and the rare cranes that court on the hill.

Forecast

Out of the fire
the bubbling blonde weathergirl
draws a cracked bone.
She holds up for the camera
bloody entrails, the ripped womb.
Smiling, she pins
over seven states the tail of an ass.
Portents be damned.
Meet me at the forum.
I'll put on the crown.

Construction

The grinding-bellied machine
leaves cement footprints
for a hundred shops in the meadow.

Weekends the pit
might be scratched Babylon:
fane and brothel
under the diggers' boots.

There was nothing here before
but the meadowlarks
and a mole trapped in the sieve.

Spread tar.
It keeps everything quiet.
In the forum we plan government
by the charred bones.

III

Aubade

The sun coughs. A stair
creaks. Before six
a neighbor descends
bearing heavily the new light in a basket.

Hospital

In the sick ward
forms hover in white.
Lights catch in the cracks of an old face.

A quick foot panics.
In that crook of sheets what's
hiding? I am wakeful in case.

I hear the feathers of nurses.
There is never enough blood to last them
before they dissolve at cockcrow.

I will rise then restored
and go out in search of a pure throat
among the village girls.

The Admiral

Near the world's edge
beyond which I can hear nothing
a dove croons
his most poignant syllable.

Old heartwringer
he is hired for the wake
for his sure grasp of infinite sorrow.

As I fall
with all my ships into the void
beyond sound and the Spanish dominions
I will carry his voice in one ear
like a circle of gold.

On Stage

When the comedian appears,
he triggers a hit song
in the violins of an ancient Rialto.

Even his detractors clap
for this whiff of sawdust.
He will not work for the laugh.

I could cry like a drunk at this schmaltz
and the memory of
those beautiful sequined disrobers.

In his blue business suit
he is an old man for all that music.
He will not let his pants fall.

Bells

In Baird's tower
the smallest bells blink.
I am growing blind
to the higher frequencies.
A beak opens and closes
on the wheeze
of a bluewinged bird,
and the unmoored dirigible carillon
sails over my head
trailing a legend: the hundred
unspeakable names of Beethoven.

Earthmoon

Moths gnaw its dowdy yellow.
It grubs my field like an old dandelion woman
gathering wine.
                    The milk horse
passes at a slow trot.
When I look out, the sky is empty.
At the full it will speak Italian.

In a space devoid of rungs
we whooped down from the cobwebbed hayloft
in our angel clothes
to the moonstraw smelling of cheddar.
When some man leaned
his tapered stairs on the cross beam
our skirts caught and we broke
like ordinary boys.

Now it sits by the street organ
combing its fur.
                    Its owl face
brings home another country.
I can talk to it with a coin.

Transfiguration

When I went down to the canoe livery,
they said he had drowned.
On the twenty-first floor he went headfirst
through the glass like a cannonball.
At the end of a screech
and black tracks on the interstate,
cops gathered his body.
He was not there either.

I saw him rising
through the bubbles of a headache commercial,
tiptoe like a rocket
with arms toward a light trolling the surface.
I saw him as the thin
bronze transvestite in breechclout,
Hiawatha-Apollo on the sunny hill
of Ohio reaching up
through the falling pollen of old firs
at the grave of the gay millionaire.

I lug him,
my deadweight of the self-destroyed,
knotted in a hobo's kerchief.
I have grappled him
from so many trout pools and airshafts.
I wear the chalk suit of his outline
on the parking lot cement.
He is not here either.

Every day I arrive
like the drycleaning delivery boy
at the back door.
He has flown off.
He has zipped on a new coverall.
He swims in a warbonnet of stars.
He knows how to leap
from the iron tentacles of a life
in the sunk hull.
I carry home his old clothes.

Burial Plot

You enter beneath seven letters of iron.
A cloud hangs in the elbow of "C".
In the house of "A" are two sparrows
and a black spider in the notch of "V".
I say to myself "CALVARY"
and think of horses.

When the horse marines came down Main Street
the tottering bugler in the grandstand
blew taps
and we took off our caps for the rough ride
up San Juan Hill
and the man on the cross Christ
torn in four by the roped Arabians.

At the end of the spike fence
you enter under the arch with its seven
wrought-iron letters of Calvary,
the place of the skull of the horse.

A Spool of Film

A scaffold vault the hall and scaffold echoes
absorbed in the echoing stitchwork of iron and iron
the crosshatch of rafters and woven trellis roof
under the roof the circus safety nets ridged
with snowfall of plaster the alpine groins of hewn
ties a rotting thicket a baffle of briar stone

I probe the mantle swaying hurdles in maze
pillars and stilts for a thatch house the spider
uprights for domes where clocks stall in grime
for an hour no better than now see how
the sky is already torn in places and lies
on the shelves of the barriers like blue eggshell
the air gnaws at the links of scaffold I climb
toward the platform where a train is due coaches
snapping their backs on the warped rails that end under
the abandoned canopy of pipes and timbers

The family waits by trackside squatting
on cardboard suitcases like immigrants the father
and mother of someone betrothed in evening clothes
huddled roosting silent as stunned pigeons fallen
on asphalt the raised walk between slivers of red
crawling steel bereaved in black feathers mother
and father and wilted child in a funeral wreath
of roses waiting the late train the pullman in splinters
locomotive awash in a flooded culvert

The tickets are in my mouth we share wedges
of German cake to pass time I chew the tickets
interred like raisins I have eaten half
the honeymoon the cake under my pillow
will ring like a liberty dollar I will pay
the traffic to Mexico on the Chief or Twilight
Limited disgorge the stubs into my hand
the tickets stuck in my teeth the sponge cake fare
while those three savor in patience my horror ancient
sequined and creased with their finery bride
who fades as the brown stays of the tumbling station
a waybill a sparrow a spool of film

Gulliver

Where are they carrying me
these small ferryman ants?
The ground is multitudes
and flows under my back.
To what pinnacle of heaped dust
or turf forest shore
of thieves tugged all smugglers
at my neck's keel? I float
on their summer scurry
lighter than booty a man
drunk on their deck of weeds.

Order of Beasts

Dragging their robes
the peacock czars climb
to a roost where all fans close
and the barbarous dancers sprawl like bears.

Cossacks gun cycles
under the camel's lip.
A claw picks at the tiger's lock
in a dungeon under the peacock stair.

Thin-necked the kings of lawn
shriek in their charnel court
and fold a spread of eyes
over stone vessels and the lion's ear.

The Shell

I hold up one house to look in.
The hinge is rigid.
The scoured halves extend like dead wings.
I peer without shame into that empty place.
I might fear life.
I might startle if the old man came to the door
with his one eye
and a gun to my chest.
These are the white walls of a lost silver town
at tidemark among crabs and sandals.

The ark fell to a worm.
Oceans trickled through the trim hole
in a forehead of chalk.
Doors burst at the knock of water.
This is the law.
The solitary shall always be hauled forth
till the heresy is expunged.
There is no place in the sea for a closed life.

Few shells here
can be heard murmuring
through their locked spiral stairs
a thrash of tides,
the backwash in a cavern.
These derelicts have no voice or echo
like the white noise of long distance
or the rustle of gowns
passing through centuries of the drafty palazzo
to the beach of Mars.

That's a whorl of nautilus
not this void.
The shell walls lean out from each other
and the gull's eye winks
at the rim of the bomb rift.
The dome of worship is gone
that coiled sound
through its rainbow of galleries.
Halves lie open where prayer lay
beating in the animal cell.
After storm you must look in the sand for churches.

I walk into the shell.
How can you say no?
I walk into the valley of the shell,
the crease between slopes of travelling ice.
The ice mountain is thin as a life
and will shatter at birdcall
if a morning can be arranged.
But here's a shale grit where trees grew
and a trickle of grass.
I walk toward the sun between frozen pinions,
wings left like a ruined ship
in the ice of the Caucasus,
the stiff wings of the falcon who gnawed
too long at the heart of the chained man
and turned to snow.
The vault is rose.
I make my own way to the sun
through shelf on shelf

of the mountain that is coming apart
like a shell at the seams.
Dawn melts through the ten cities of Troy
to the deepest color.
Grosbeaks in a canyon
sing with their breasts on fire.

I hold in my hand this one house.
I am empty outside.
Seaweed could make a latch.
Why cover us?
There are still stars awhile to weave roofing.
A palm leaf.
I think of a captain who sweat years
to hoist sail through a bottle's neck,
how he raised
mast on mast of his toothpick sloop
to weigh full-rigged
on the green seas of his flask.
At launch he steadied her deck
with his two feet on the fragile planking.
Grain on grain
he had built himself all beard
and thar-she-blows into his own
perfect ship.
This hall is mine.
I will sing in these walls a household
against any cold, once again
the animal within.

North

Clouds are coming out of the sun. Bees issue from the roadside
gentian. Objects are brought to labor who have known
none of their own kind.

Anger eludes me. It comes from another's mouth and I recognize
what I have not said. I am the receptacle for such
oblique favors.

The crow saws a path from birch to elm, a heaving loud
body proclaiming his apprehensions. He has beaten back
even the humid air that sorries a cat.

Called a run, it flows through a cleft in the city. The sense
of meander is an art. A sound of pebbles emerges.

I live in a crack in the mountain and have forgotten the
simplest oracles. Do not come to me for solutions. I
know north but not why.

IV

Letter Beyond the World

When books burn
the words fuse in one scream.
The Alexandrian libraries collapse
into a bullet hole,
the black draft in a wind sock.

I send this plaque aloft
with the cipher of Idaho
and the names of the deities
Topeka and Cheyenne.
This is our calendar stone.

You who detect
the months Macon and Baltimore,
it was not all mayhem.
Times we died
simply for love of each other.

I have scriven these lists
to remind you of songbirds.
My name will not translate.
Call me Interstate.
Or Bad Axe.

The Museum of Tucumcari

The little saws of agave
pry a grey sawdust from the buckboard.
Sand grains like the lead of badmen
bore worm holes. The wagon tongue
drips among cairns and a third milestone
points to the plumbing.

They have turned the schoolyard into a lesson.
The mesa is docked
like Old Ironsides at the tollgate.
And the reel ends
with the cavalry pinned down
behind their ornamented saddles.

At the back gate
beyond the hand pumps and opuntia
a privy gapes. I am humbled
by these arts and landmarks
of the white experience.

Cowboy Museum

What is lacking are hoofbeats,
the stink of broncs.
I touch a wax calf.
The horned animal roars from his chute
into the stop-frame
of cement halls and church architecture.

Once I saw Buffalo Bill
with his counterfeit white hair.
He fired blanks, he split
clay platters in mid-air.
A brass band led the stampede.

In this clean shrine guards hush
irreverent children.
A diffused light shuns the redskin dead.
Why are we talking in whispers?
Priez pour nous, John Wayne.

Palo Duro

The cliffs are stippled with new beard.
Between my feet my own
shadow crouches in a wide hat.
Discarded gods whose names escape me
are stacked with the bunny-ears
and the seared paloburger.
I will certainly not ride a child's toy railway
exposed to the hook-nosed
red shafts. I refuse to be awed
by sexual pinnacles, brazen crags,
or the florid, pocked, tumid sandstone.
I can clatter these palings with a dry stick
or scrawl obscenities with a jackhammer!

Why am I cold?
I sit down under the cottonwoods.
I drink a chilled beer from the fliptop
but the rocks crowd me.
They are coming over the road with impassive,
masked faces like priests
of an outlawed order. I begin to count
assets, a column of sums, five fingers.
The woodpecker with a golden forehead shrieks
from the crumbling treetrunk.
I take off my shoes. I count my toes.
I crawl between my bare feet growing heavier.
I pretend to be stone.

Safari

The air is wheat.
Teeth grit on the least words
and the heat gauge mires
in a red zone.
We bog among yellow roaring animals
at a roadblock.
Lions circle Abilene.

The fence that strung hawks
from the hawkbeds of Colorado
is devoured
by the storm-lunged cattle.
The earth is moved.
The earth is moving over.
The barbed wire curls in my stomach.

But here come lovers
or saviors in a dust haze: girls
in T-shirts of hot pink
and green fatigues.
Their tropical hats bob
like white anglers' floats.
They are tamers

and road women deep
in grins of sun oil.
They wave us oneway
into the detours with neon wands
and brown arms.
They are cool in turmoil.
This is my love zone.

Perspective

Hawks knob each
fifth phone pole in the descending
ranks, road and wire
shrink toward the pursed end
and if we are no smaller then
we will trip
on hawks and fences
and slam into the grey sky hung
between us and Missouri.

Pueblo

Above the dust
and mud bricks melting
into the creek bed and cracked earth
like a candle
the dirt dam
wedged between scrub and scrub
reins back
what is left of the yellow water.

There are no people below the shadow
except these earth people
who thirst
who paint in the clay a black eagle
a glazed eye
and a red god.
Their dogs with ribs like rake prongs
groan
in the dry cataracts of dream.

The high dam keeps
in its deep vaults
the algebra of fish.
Sign by sign the lake grows
in the soundings of hired wizards
who pray
in their private mornings to the dark lord
of wheels and iron.

Until they go higher
the earth people will get less,
until they move
into the government hills
or the sewers of the white city
they will rattle like pods.
Feathered kachina
will not answer the rain dance,
they wear
the tin hats of engineers.

Mark as crop
a yield of raw coals.
The round chambers have baked
grit and the smoulder
of failed vines. May the earth
break and the lake fling
its outboards and fishermen
downstream. Let them pass
these houses shouting.

The old wrap themselves from the sun.
If a wind comes
they will flutter and snap off
at the stem. They wrap themselves
in the color of ash
and eagles, in the weave
of parched rimrock and red clay.
They begin again.

Heat Wave in Quinter, Kansas

If we touch,
my hands will break off.
We are so naked
we are neither man nor woman.

Those lovers raked
through the high rings of inferno
flared at a kiss.
I have observed their incandescence.

In the night fields
combines spew their gold fountains of chaff.
Hide your body.
It is fragile as wheat.

Kiva

Windows admit emptiness.
Lamp and broom
scratch the fireblack cave ceiling.
The walls are called Those Who Fled.

Four claws carried them off.
The light on a bony horse
pierced the open doorway.
The arrow said Old Ones.

I go down a ladder
into the warm community.
There are no windows in this house,
only peace, myself, and those others.

This book
was composed and
printed at Ithaca House
Press by J. Marc Freedman.